Minutes a Day-Mastery for a Lifetime!

Level 7

English Grammar & Writing Mechanics

Nancy McGraw & Nancy Tondy

Bright Ideas Press, LLC
Cleveland, OH

Summer Solutions Level 7
English Grammar & Writing Mechanics

All rights reserved. No part of this publication may be reproduced or transmitted in any form or by any means, electronic or mechanical, including photocopy, recording, or any information storage or retrieval system. Reproduction of these materials for an entire class, school, or district is prohibited.

Printed in the United States of America

ISBN: 978-1-934210-08-6

Cover Design: Dan Mazzola
Editor: Kimberly A. Dambrogio
Randy Reetz
Illustrator: Christopher Backs

Copyright © 2011 by Bright Ideas Press, LLC
Cleveland, Ohio

Instructions for Parents/Guardians

- *Summer Solutions* is an extension of the *Simple Solutions* Approach being used by thousands of children in schools across the United States.

- The 30 lessons included in each workbook are meant to review and reinforce the skills learned in the grade level just completed.

- The program is designed to be used three days per week for ten weeks to ensure retention.

- Completing the book all at one time defeats the purpose of sustained practice over the summer break.

- Each book contains answers for each lesson.

- Each book contains Help Pages which list vocabulary, parts of speech, editing marks, rules for capitalization, punctuation, and spelling.

- Lessons should be checked immediately for optimal feedback.

- Adjust the use of the book to fit vacations. More lessons may have to be completed during the weeks before or following a family vacation.

Summer Solutions Level 7
English Grammar & Writing Mechanics

Reviewed Skills Include

- The Writing Process
- Sentence Structure
- All Parts of Speech
- Verb Types and Subject-Verb Agreement
- Conjugation of Regular and Irregular Verbs
- Capitalization, Punctuation, and Spelling Rules
- Greek and Latin Roots
- Synonyms, Antonyms, Homophones, and Homographs
- Connotation and Denotation
- Context Clues
- Cause and Effect
- Metaphors and Similes
- Fact and Opinion
- Analogies
- Bibliography Citations

Help Pages begin on page 63.

Answers to Lessons begin on page 73.

Lesson #1

1. Use context clues to select the meaning of the underlined word.

    Although there was no visible damage to the first floor, the <u>dank</u> basement carpet was clearly the result of a flood.

    perceptible   below ground   dehydrated   damp

In an inverted sentence, the subject comes after the verb.

   Example: In the back of the room (are) plenty of extra chairs.
                                    main verb   complete subject

   (*Plenty of extra chairs are* in the back of the room.)

   The next two sentences have inverted order. Circle each verb and underline each complete subject.

2. Under the Christmas tree lay the most unique train set Brian had ever seen.

3. Near the outskirts of town lived a lonely little troll.

4. Use a dictionary to determine which word is a synonym for the word *disparity*.

    similarity   anguish   difference   elation

5. **Compound nouns are made up of more than one word, and they come in three forms: proper nouns** (Mrs. Hewes, Eaton Park), **hyphenated words** (mayor-elect), **and separate words** (truck driver, tortoise shell).

   Underline all the compound nouns.

   Our tour guide suggested using the online option to get tickets to Zany World.

6. Add -*ly* to these adjectives to form adverbs; write them below.

   complete ➔ _____   gradual ➔ _____   chief ➔ _____

7. Write the principle parts of the verb *swell*. Check the *Help Pages* for irregular verbs.

Present	Past	Present Participle	Past Participle

8. Add commas to separate the series of adjectives in the following sentence.

   During the debate, all of the mayoral candidates appeared intelligent honest friendly and competent.

9. Remember, *connotation* is the tone of a word. Choose the word that you think has the most positive connotation.

   When traveling alone, it's a good idea to be (suspicious / distrustful / cautious).

10. The pronoun and verb do not agree with the antecedent in the following sentence. Cross out the pronoun and verb; write them correctly on the line.

    The school has high standards, but they do not require an entry exam.

    _____

11 – 12. **Identify the Sentence Parts**   Match each of the underlined sentence parts with its name below.

<u>Our</u> <u>greatest</u> natural <u>resource</u> <u>is</u> the <u>minds</u> of our <u>children</u>. –Walt Disney
 A   B   C   D   E   F

_____ predicate noun   _____ object of a preposition   _____ subject

_____ linking verb   _____ possessive pronoun   _____ adjective

Lesson #2

1. **Interrogative sentences have inverted order.**
   Example: Is anyone eating breakfast today?   (*Anyone is eating breakfast today.*)
               verb subject verb
   Underline the simple subject; write the verb phrase.

   Are you traveling this weekend?   _____

2. Underline the compound nouns.

   You can get a weather update about Death Valley in the "Morning Report."

3. **An adverb clause modifies a verb, adjective or another adverb.**
   Example: Please watch your sister *until I get home.* (The adverb clause modifies *watch*.)
   Underline the adverb clause.

   You can relax as long as there are no customers.

4. What does an adverb clause modify?   _____

5. Complete the analogy.

   angle : geometry : : lightning : _____

   A) thunder   B) weather   C) sky   D) rain

6. **Use commas to set off <u>non-restrictive modifiers</u> (unnecessary words or phrases).**
   Example: Mrs. Bloom, one of our neighbors, is the head nurse.
   Insert commas.

   The marathon an annual event is sponsored by Mack's Pizzeria.

7. Look in the *Help Pages* for suggestions as to how to fix a run-on sentence. Then correctly rewrite the sentence below.

   Luke had been to many summer camps before he knew there were rules and sometimes the food was lousy but he always had fun because he made friends and besides being away from his little sisters was a nice break plus Luke enjoyed all the outdoor camp activities like canoeing and rock climbing.

   _____
   _____
   _____
   _____

Complete the conjugation of the verb *dive* in all 14 tenses, using *Seals* as the subject.

		Past	Present	Future
8.	Basic	Seals dove.		
9.	Perfect			Seals will have dived.
10.	Progressive	Seals were diving.		
11.	Perfect Progressive		Seals have been diving.	
12.	Emphatic			---

Lesson #3

1. What is the meaning of the Greek root in all three of these words?

    monocle   monopoly   monodrama

    _____ together   _____ one, or single   _____ new

2. Use editing marks to correct four capitalization errors.

    Last Spring, my Mom surprised grandpa with an alaskan husky puppy.

3. Choose the correct words to complete the sentence.

    Cheryl did (poor / poorly) on the test; she said many of the questions were (challenging / challengingly).

4. Underline the verb. Then rewrite the sentence using the passive voice of the verb.

    Ken lit the candles.

    _____

5. Place a comma after the introductory adverb clause.

    As long as there is no lightning we can stay on the golf course.

6. Use a dictionary to check the spelling of these plurals. If a word is misspelled, cross it out and write it correctly on the line.

    tattoos _____ memo's _____ hooves _____

7. Underline the relative pronoun and circle its antecedent.

    The lady with whom you arrived is waiting for you in the gift shop.

8. Is the underlined clause subordinate or independent?

    <u>Ever since the new highway was completed</u>, businesses in the area have been flourishing.

    subordinate   independent

9. Choose an antonym which will change the meaning of the sentence.

   Members of the team communicate with each other using covert symbols.

   clear   ancient   complex   secret

10 – 12. Look at the graphic organizer below, and use the information to write three cause-effect statements about malnutrition. Try to use cause-effect signal words.

   caused by   therefore   since   then   due to

   may cause   as a result   leads to   so   because

Causes of Malnutrition	Effects of Malnutrition
• not eating enough food • eating foods that are not nutritious • inability to digest food and/or inability to absorb nutrients	• low weight; stunted growth • illness • poor brain function • weak muscles, fragile bones • decaying teeth

_____

_____

_____

_____

_____

_____

_____

_____

Lesson #4

1. Fix this run-on by inserting a semicolon between the two independent clauses.

    Vince tried out for football and made the team as soon as football season was over, he wanted to try out for basketball.

2. **In a compound noun, the first word may modify the second.**
   Example: a <u>library</u> <u>book</u>
   (*Library* modifies *book*. Hence, *library* is a <u>noun</u> used as an <u>adjective</u>.)
   Underline the compound nouns. Draw a second line under noun modifiers.

    The ballet teacher ordered a carrot cake to serve at the dance recital.

3. Underline the transitive verb, circle the indirect object, and put a box around the direct object.

    The entire audience gave the drummers a standing ovation.

4. Underline the adverb clause; then add a comma.

    Until I graduated from high school I was not allowed to own a car.

5. Underline two synonyms in the sentence.

    At the vendor fair, the most prosperous business owners vie for the attention of affluent customers.

6. Choose the words that correctly complete the sentence.

    (It's / Its) not (two / to / too) cold for tent camping as long as you (where / wear / ware) warm clothing.

7. Underline the indefinite pronoun, and choose the pronoun that agrees.

   Everyone needs to show (her / their) passport and airline ticket.

8. Choose the item which has the softest connotation.

   It is (foul / impolite / vulgar) to begin speaking when someone is speaking to you.

9. The following sentence contains an *implied* metaphor. To what is the sunset view being compared?

   The sky was ablaze with the brilliant colors of a summer sunset.

   _____

10. Rewrite this opinion as a fact.

    The best place for your money is in a savings account.

    _____
    _____
    _____

11 – 12. **Identify the Sentence Parts**

   <u>On August 15th</u>, <u>our football training camp begins</u>, <u>so</u>
        A   B   C

   I <u>will be running</u> laps at the track every morning.
            D

   _____ conjunction

   _____ main clause

   _____ adverb phrase that tells *when*

   _____ future progressive tense verb

Lesson #5

1. Rewrite this run-on correctly. (See the *Help Pages*.)

    On the hottest days of summer, the firefighters like to open fire hydrants kids splash through the running water.

    _____

    _____

2. Underline the compound nouns; put a double line under those that act as modifiers.
   Example: All <u>soccer</u> <u>coaches</u> recommend carrying <u>water</u> <u>bottles</u>.

    The café owner brought us apple pie.

3. Underline the adverb phrase that tells *when*. What word does the adverb phrase modify?

    I look for rainbows after a storm. _____

4. Add the <u>past perfect form</u> of the verb *rake*.

    Lorraine was able to plant the tulip bulbs since Patti _____ _____

    all the flower beds.

5. Add the necessary commas to this sentence.

    The airline offers a snack not a meal to passengers flying in the afternoon.

6. Choose the correct pronoun.

    Mrs. Greely didn't ask (whose / who's) turn it was.

7. Use editing marks to correct three capitalization errors.

    On easter Sunday grandma serves cornish hens with all the trimmings.

8 – 11. The writing selection below contains some errors. Evaluate the selection, and follow the directions in the checklist.

Colleges offer summer programs to seventh and eighth graders for a variety of reasons. One purpose of these programs are to expose students to coarses that may not be available at their middle schools. Like robotics or debate. Traditional summer camps focus on outdoor recreation, team building, crafts, and the envirament. Some kids actually prefers academic experiences, so the college and university sessions usually focus on academics. Also, these programs provide a "dorm experience" which allow kids to see what it's like to be a college student. And a chance to meet other kids like themselves. One more reason colleges and universities invite middle school students to spend a week or two on campus is to ensure that students include higher education in their future plans.

_____ Underline the topic sentence.

_____ Does every sentence express a complete thought and include a subject and a verb? Draw a line through any fragments.

_____ Does each sentence have subject-verb agreement? If not, cross out the incorrect verb(s) and add the correct ones, using the editing mark for "add something."

_____ Are all the words spelled correctly? If not, use the editing mark for "check spelling" to mark them.

12. According to the selection, which of these is not a reason that colleges and universities offer summer programs to middle school students?

       A) These programs are required by law.

       B) The programs provide a "dorm experience."

       C) The programs offer courses not available at some local middle schools.

       D) The programs give kids the opportunity to meet other like-minded kids.

Lesson #6

1. Add two editing marks to show how the run-on could be written as two sentences.

    Lucille has a recipe for fried bananas her recipe includes chocolate chips and shredded coconut.

2. Underline the compound nouns; put a double line under the nouns that act as modifiers.

    The copy machine was repaired by a technology specialist.

3. Underline the adverb clause. What word does the adverb clause modify?

    Nettie told a story while she stirred the pudding. _____

4. A) Which type of verb is active?

    _____ transitive   _____ intransitive   _____ both

    B) Which type of verb has a direct object?

    _____ transitive   _____ intransitive   _____ both

5. Rewrite the two sentences as a single sentence with an appositive.

    The Wilsons' house is a two-story colonial. The Wilsons' house has a full basement.

    _____

    _____

6. Use editing marks to show any word that should be capitalized.

    Yesterday dad caught a walleye at jefferson lake.

7. Complete this analogy.   lifeguard : water park : : _____

   A) security guard : stadium   C) umpire : baseball
   B) coach : swimmer   D) clerk : toy store

8. Match these word parts with their meanings. Use a dictionary if you need to.

   A) *mono-*   B) *amphi-*   C) *neo-*

   _____ new   _____ one   _____ both

9. Choose the verb that agrees.

   When we (was / were) learning the algorithms, we practiced them every day.

10. Underline the complete subject.

    All of the baby zoo animals are filmed as part of a research study.

11. Circle two errors in the sentence; then rewrite the sentence correctly.

    Take your cell phone incase any of yous need to call home.

    _____

    _____

12. Rewrite the following sentence correctly.

    Doing odd jobs, mowing lawns, and babysitting are just a few of the ways to ~~If you~~ earn extra cash this summer.

    _____

    _____

    _____

Lesson #7

1. What is a linking verb? Put a check next to any phrase that describes a linking verb. (Find this information in the *Help Pages*.)

   _____ shows action   _____ does not show action

   _____ includes all forms of *be*   _____ is transitive

2. Make a list of five linking verbs. _____

   _____

3. **Remember, a linking verb connects the subject to a predicate nominative, which** *renames* **the subject.**
   Example: Nicholas became the leader.
                 subject   linking verb   predicate nominative

   Circle the linking verb; underline the predicate nominative.

   Lake Erie is their home, and pollution threatens to destroy it.

4. Choose the correct word to modify the verb.

   We have to walk quite a distance, so travel (light / lightly).

5. The following selection contains a simile or a metaphor; which is it? Underline the two things being compared.

   The room was as warm as an oven once the furnace was lit.

   simile   metaphor

6. Underline the verb(s) in this sentence; circle the simple subject. (Pay attention to inverted order.)

   Did you send a text message to your teacher?

7. Cross out the reflexive pronoun that is used incorrectly; write the correct pronoun above it.

   Someone as old as yourself should definitely have a savings account.

8. Fill in the present perfect tense of the verb *win*.

   Our softball team _____ the regional championship for the past three years.

9. Use what you know about prefixes and roots to match these words with their meanings.

   A) portage   ____ the act of carrying

   B) biennial   ____ measures time

   C) chronometer   ____ every two years

10. Decide whether each sentence states a fact or an opinion. Then write F for fact or O for opinion on the line next to each sentence.

    A) ____ Peer pressure is one of the toughest issues facing middle school students today.

    B) ____ In a recent poll of 13-year-olds, 22% stated that "peer group approval" was more important to them than "parent approval."

11 – 12. **Identify the Sentence Parts**

   <u>Peer pressure</u> can also be <u>positive</u>. You are <u>applying</u> a form of
       A   B   C

   <u>positive</u> peer pressure <u>whenever</u> you <u>advise</u> a <u>friend</u> to do the right thing.
     D   E   F   G

   _____ predicate adjective   _____ present progressive tense

   _____ adjective   _____ direct object

   _____ transitive verb   _____ subject

   _____ subordinating conjunction

Lesson #8

Review these prefixes by placing them correctly in the chart. Then write an example of a word with each prefix.

ante-   trans-   anti-

	Prefix	Meaning	Example
1.		across	
2.		against	
3.		before	

4. Remember, an adverb phrase is a prepositional phrase which modifies a verb, adjective, or adverb. Underline the adverb phrase.

   Patrick and I kept cracking up during our rehearsal.

5. Underline the adverb clause that tells *why*. What word does the clause modify?

   Adjust the window blinds so that the room is shaded.   _____

6. **Verbs may be *active* or *passive*. In the *active voice* the verb sends its action to a direct object. Example**: <u>Volunteers</u> <u>painted</u> the <u>building</u>.
                 subject   verb   direct object

   In the *passive voice*, the subject is acted upon.
   Example: The <u>building</u> <u>was painted</u> <u>by volunteers</u>.
           subject past participle prepositional phrase

   Write A if the verb is active; write P if it is passive.

   _____ Popular new breakfast breads are made by Emil's Bakery.

   _____ People buy the breads as fast as Emil can bake them.

7. Punctuate this sentence. Add three commas, an apostrophe, and an end mark.

   Okay cover art can be submitted but it s due by Wednesday April 10

8. Underline two antonyms in the sentence.

   If yearbook sales are to be profitable this year, we need to order an abundant supply; last year, the copies were scarce.

9. Underline the transitive verb, circle the indirect object, and put a box around the direct object.

   Our advisor gave Glenda six digital photos for the yearbook.

10. Choose the verb that agrees.

    Neither outdoor camping nor rock climbing (is / are) my first choice.

11. Sort the nouns into two categories: singular and plural.

    donuts   license   clouds   forest   people   weather

    Singular - _____

    Plural - _____

12. When Gisele was writing her essay, she used a book called *Careers in Gaming* by Walter Shock. The book was published in Toronto in 2006 by Roulette Press. Show how Gisele should cite this reference. Read the *Help Pages* to learn how to cite a reference.

    _____

    _____

    _____

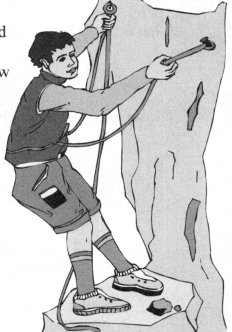

Lesson #9

1. For each of the following sentences, write whether the adverb phrase tells how, when, where, why, or to what extent.

    A) We moved before the first of August. _____

    B) Our new house was far from the city. _____

    C) I travel to school by bus. _____

    D) I ride my bike as much as possible. _____

Sort the nouns into two categories: common and proper. (If the noun is proper, begin it with a capital letter.)

    louise   power   raisins   mr. norris   virginia   tricycle

2. Common - _____

3. Proper - _____

4. Add the present perfect form of the verb *shed*.

    Once the snake _____ _____ its skin, it will be very thirsty.

5. What is the structure of the sentence written below?   simple   compound   complex

    Now that the new water park is open, we can have my birthday party there!

6. The sentence below has inverted order. Underline the verb; circle the simple subject.

    In the entryway hangs a magnificent painting.

7. Write A if the verb is active; write P if it is passive.

    _____ Sierra wore a white tee shirt and brought a handful of multi-colored markers on the last day of school.

    _____ By the end of the day, Sierra's tee shirt was decorated with the colorful signatures of everyone in her class.

8 – 12. Read this babysitter's description of a very rough day. Then complete the cause-effect organizer with the chain reaction of events described in the story.

One winter day I was babysitting my neighbor's children. All of a sudden, their cat began climbing up the Christmas tree, and the tree started to fall. I lunged across the room and caught the tree before it hit the ground. But part of the tree stand bent when the tree tipped forward, so I couldn't get it to stand up on its own. Using my foot, I pushed on the stand to try to straighten it, but I just shook the whole tree. The shaking spooked the cat and it jumped off, knocking over a cup of lemonade that one of the kids had left on the coffee table. What a mess there was!

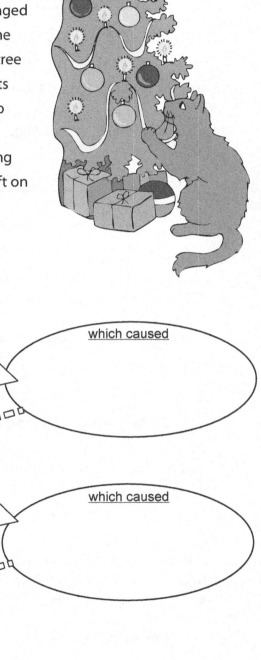

Starting Event

which caused

which caused

which caused

which caused

Lesson #10

1. Fix this run-on sentence by inserting a comma and a coordinating conjunction between the two independent clauses. Rewrite the sentence below.

    Flip-flops are comfortable it isn't sensible to wear them in the winter.
    _____
    _____

2. Sort the nouns into two categories: abstract and concrete.

    devotion   hot dogs   confidence   safety   magazine   camel

    Abstract - _____
    Concrete - _____

3. Look at this sentence: Renee and Kenny modeled teen clothing at the fashion show. What is the best way to rewrite the sentence with the passive voice of the verb?

    A) At the fashion show, Renee and Kenny had modeled teen clothing.
    B) Teen clothing was modeled by Renee and Kenny at the fashion show.
    C) Renee and Kenny are modeling teen clothing at the fashion show.
    D) Renee and Kenny did model teen clothing at the fashion show.

4. Add a colon and three commas.

    Mandy wants to try everything canoeing skiing biking and horseback riding.

5. The sentence below contains a simile or metaphor. Which is it? Underline the two things being compared.

    Hope is the air we breathe.

    simile   metaphor

6. Complete this analogy.   jeopardy : risk : : _____

   A) young : aged   C) vast : massive
   B) Monopoly : game   D) broccoli : green

7. What is the meaning of the Latin root shared by all of the words listed below?

   _____

   omnipotent   omnibus   omnivore   omnipresent   omniscient

8. Which spelling is correct?   locally   localy

9. Locate the antecedent and choose the pronoun that agrees.

   The herd searched for shelter and food for (its / their) young.

10 – 12. Read the following selection. Then complete the graphic organizer by placing a check mark in each category that applies to the underlined verbs. The first one has been done for you.

   Camouflage clothing <u>was</u> created for the military, but now it's a popular fashion trend with both boys and girls. You <u>will</u> see boys wearing the darker colors like greens and browns, whereas girls <u>go</u> for the blues, pinks, and oranges. Camouflage colored scarves or bandanas <u>are</u> great for everyone. These fabrics <u>give</u> kids a stylish look; they <u>look</u> fun and flattering.

Verb	Action	Helping	Linking	Past	Present	Future
was		✓		✓		
will						
go						
are						
give						
look						

Lesson #11

1. Use context clues to choose the meaning of the underlined word.

    Sandra had many excuses for the things that went wrong in the office, but her explanations were tenuous, and the boss began to doubt Sandra's reliability.

    A) dependable   B) creative   C) exaggerated   D) questionable

2. Correct any capitalization errors with the proper editing marks.

    We visited the hoover dam and lake mead while we were in nevada.

3. **Choosing the word with the best connotation will make your writing smooth.**
    A word with the wrong connotation will clash with your writing. Choose the best word.

    Trudy's brother likes to photograph interesting and (unusual / abnormal) buildings.

4. The following selection contains a simile or a metaphor; which is it? Underline the two things being compared.

    The storage room was a museum for childhood memories,

    yard sale leftovers, and items of unknown origin.

    simile   metaphor

5. Add the past perfect form of the verb *forget*.

    By the time the movie ended, Phyllis

    _____ _____

    about her quarrel with Susanna.

6. Circle the linking verb; underline the action verb.

    The playground is unsafe, so a security guard locked the gates.

7. Is the action verb in the sentence above transitive or intransitive?

    transitive   intransitive

8. Indicate whether each statement is a fact or an opinion.

   A) _____ The Occupational Safety and Health Administration (OSHA) is a government agency that enforces standards to protect the health and safety of teen-aged workers.

   B) _____ Having a summer job will teach you responsibility and give you some of the skills you will need to be successful in life.

9 – 12. Many young people would like to earn money by having part-time jobs. However, anyone under 14 years of age is not eligible for a work permit. Even with a permit, there are restrictions that limit both the number of hours teens can work and the types of jobs they can hold. Are these restrictions a good idea? Give your opinion and back it up with an explanation.

_____

_____

_____

_____

_____

_____

_____

_____

_____

Lesson #12

1. List the three perfect forms of the verb *seek*. Use the subject *We*.

    Past perfect - _____

    Present perfect - _____

    Future perfect - _____

2. Complete this analogy.

    post office : stamps :: café : _____

    A) meal   B) eat   C) mail   D) restaurant

3. Is the underlined word used as an adjective or a noun?

    Aunt Lisa's lungs are irritated by <u>minute</u> dust particles.

    adjective   noun

4. Match these word parts with their meanings. Use a dictionary if you need help.

    A) *hemi-*   B) *biblio-*   C) *photo-*

    _____ book   _____ light   _____ half

5. Rewrite the two sentences as a single sentence with an appositive.

    My favorite breakfast is on the menu. My favorite breakfast is French toast.

    _____

    _____

6. Make the sentence clearer by crossing out the pronoun and replacing it with a noun.

    Don's puppy likes to keep him company while he is reading.

7. Which of these is a subordinate clause? _____

<u>If the pitcher is successful</u>, <u>our opponent won't score enough runs to win the game</u>.
        A   B

8. Choose the word that correctly completes the sentence.

    Larry agrees with (your / you're) description of the concert.

9. Underline the relative pronoun and dependent clause in this sentence.

    The room was filled with computers that were not even functional.

10. Correct two capitalization errors with the proper editing marks.

    My Grandmother served german chocolate cake with vanilla ice cream.

11 – 12. **Identify the Sentence Parts**
Match each of the underlined sentence parts with its name below.

    The Evergreen State College, located in the <u>beautiful</u> Pacific Northwest,
                                                                 A

<u>offers</u> environmental <u>education</u>, and <u>its</u> students <u>participate</u> in many
  B   C   D   E

green <u>activities</u>.
         F

_____ direct object

_____ intransitive verb

_____ transitive verb

_____ possessive pronoun

_____ adjective

_____ object of a preposition

Lesson #13

1. Write A if the verb is active; write P if it is passive.

   _____ The newspaper was delivered early this morning.

   _____ But I haven't had a chance to read it yet.

2. What is the <u>denotation</u> of the word <u>heart</u>?

   A) spirit   B) valentine   C) feeling   D) internal organ

3. Use what you know about prefixes and roots to match these words with their meanings.

   _____ circumvent   A) study of time

   _____ chronology   B) writing

   _____ script   C) go around

4. Which spelling is correct?

   _____ Feburary   _____ February

   _____ neither   _____ both

5. Choose the verb that agrees.

   The picnic basket, along with all the leftovers, (is / are) in the pavilion.

6. Underline the compound nouns.

   Mr. Holmes brought his Olympic medal to our day camp.

7. Which of these is an independent clause? _____

<u>Now that the storm has passed</u>, <u>we can go into the water</u>
　　　　A　　　　　　　　　　　　　B

<u>as long as it isn't too cold</u>.
　　　　C

Conjugate the irregular verb *strike* in all 14 tenses, using *The batter* as the subject.

		Past	Present	Future
8.	Basic			
9.	Perfect			
10.	Progressive			
11.	Perfect Progressive			
12.	Emphatic			---

Lesson #14

1. Write the principle parts of the verb *pay*. Check the *Help Pages* if you are not sure.

Present	Past	Present Participle	Past Participle

2. Underline two antonyms in this sentence.

   Toni ordered a colossal ice cream sundae; however, she has a petite appetite, so we all ate some of the scrumptious dessert.

3. Find the word *phenomena* in a dictionary. What is its singular form?

   _____

4. What is the meaning of *phenomena*?

   A) monsters   B) time   C) happenings   D) miracles

5. Correct any capitalization errors using the proper editing marks.

   She was carrying a book titled the golden compass.

6. Choose the correct pronoun.

   With (who / whom) did you make arrangements?

7. Decide whether the indefinite pronouns are singular or plural, and choose the verbs that agree.

   <u>Most</u> of the news (was / were) good, but <u>none</u> of the statistics (was / were) given.

8. Homer wants to use information from the book *Landscaping Careers* by Daisy Gardens. The book was published in Chicago in 2006 by Greens Press. Show how Homer should cite this reference.

   _____

   _____

9. Choose the correct word to complete the sentence.

   Run (quick / quickly) and get our rain gear out of the tent.

10. Combine the verbs with a conjunction and write a single sentence.

    Mason is on the student council. Mason wants to be class president.

    _____

    _____

Read each sentence, and label it simple, compound, complex, or compound-complex. Check the *Help Pages* if you don't remember which is which.

11. Whenever Susan is in charge, we have to clean our rooms, and we aren't allowed to use the telephone.

    _____

12. Susan is a little bossy, but she's very responsible.

    _____

Lesson #15

1. Use context clues to match the meaning of the underlined word.

    Amory's <u>acerbic</u> description of his week at Camp Kuruk made us cringe; he really hated everything about the camp.

    amusing   clever   charming   bitter

2. Add the <u>future perfect form</u> of the verb *hang*.

    I'm hoping that my sister _____ _____ _____ all the decorations, so we can work on refreshments.

3. Complete the chart by filling in the correct spelling next to each mispronounced or misspelled word. One has been done for you.

Mispronounced/Misspelled Words	Correct Spelling
alot	
dis	this
drownd	
probly	

4. Choose the correct verbs.

    An afternoon of swimming or a hike in the park (burn / burns) calories and (promote / promotes) fitness.

5. Underline the demonstrative. Is it used as a pronoun or an adjective?

    You should open this before you call Hillary.

    pronoun   adjective

6. Choose the verb that agrees.

    An army of volunteers (has / have) refurbished the entire building.

7. Is the underlined part of the sentence a phrase or a clause?

    The letter <u>must have gotten lost</u> on the way to its destination.

    phrase   clause

8. Underline a prepositional phrase; circle the object of the preposition.

   Try not to go over any large stones with the lawn mower.

Find an error in each of the following sentences. Cross out the error and write the correction above it.

   Example: Your work is beautiful; you did ~~good~~ well!

9. Mom made some sandwiches for yourself and Tory.

10. When you was in fifth grade, Sr. Ann Marie was your teacher.

11. The zoo opens it's gates at 10:00 a.m., but some of the exhibits don't open until noon.

12. All of the girls are petite, but Millie is the smaller of the three.

Lesson #16

1. List the three <u>perfect progressive forms</u> of the verb *mop*. Use the subject *He*.

   A) _____

   B) _____

   C) _____

2. Complete this analogy.   crust : pie : : _____

   A) fruit : apple   C) ingredient : bake

   B) lean : healthy   D) roof : building

3. Match these word parts with their meanings.

   _____ -ology   _____ centri-   _____ micro-

   A) small   B) study   C) center

4. The following selection contains a simile or a metaphor; which is it? Underline the two things being compared.

   With no furniture or art in the room, each wall was a blank canvas.

   simile   metaphor

5. Choose the correct verbs.

   A tall glass of orange juice or lemonade (taste / tastes) great and (supply / supplies) you with plenty of vitamin C.

6. Add *-ly* to these adjectives; write the adverbs below.

   astute → _____

   logical → _____

   lucky → _____

7. Correct any capitalization errors with the proper editing marks.

   Wendy said, "let's get an italian ice and sit under that shady tree."

8. Cross out the reflexive pronoun that is used incorrectly; replace it with the correct pronoun.

   Brandon nearly gave hisself a concussion with that boomerang!

9. Choose the verb that agrees with the collective noun.

   The Senate (adjourn / adjourns) its meetings over the holiday weekend.

10. **An adjective clause modifies a noun or a pronoun.**
    Choose the word that the adjective clause modifies.

    The winds *that knocked down the power lines* also blew off part of our roof.

11. Roseanne used information from the article "Claustrophobia" which she found in the 2001 edition of *Minds Encyclopedia*. It was on page 33 of volume two. Show how Roseanne should cite this reference.

    _____

    _____

12. Use two editing marks to correct errors in the following sentence.

    The Olympics were held in China that year, and I got to go their that Summer.

Lesson #17

1. Write the principle parts of the verb *upset*. Check the *Help Pages* if you need to.

Present	Past	Present Participle	Past Participle

2. Choose the word that you think has the softest connotation.

   It is (vulgar / rude / impolite) not to remove your shoes before entering the yoga studio.

3. Add commas.

   The bouquet was made with lilies carnations roses and ferns.

4. Use what you know about prefixes and roots to match these words with their meanings.

   ____ microphotograph   A) middle point of view

   ____ centrism   B) the study of secrets

   ____ cryptology   C) tiny picture

5. Choose the verb that agrees.

   The African countries of Senegal, Mauritania, and the Gambia (are / is) bordered by the Atlantic Ocean.

6. Is the verb in the sentence above active or passive?

   active   passive

7. Match each underlined part with its function in the sentence.

   When you say, "Ohio," you are speaking a greeting in the Japanese language.
           A   B   C

   _____ verb phrase   _____ prepositional phrase

   _____ subordinate clause

8. Cross out the incorrect pronoun and verb; write the correct pronoun and verb on the line.

   The Corners Café is a great place to eat because they serve breakfast all day.

   _____

9. Write C for clause or P for phrase.

   _____ over the crosswalk   _____ if we succeed

10. Underline the adjective clause. What noun does the clause modify?

    The music that we heard was a bagpipe melody.

    _____

Read each sentence, and label it as simple, compound, complex, or compound-complex. Check the *Help Pages* if you don't remember which is which.

11. "Before you criticize someone, you should walk a mile in his shoes.

    _____

12. That way, when you criticize him, you are a mile away, and you have his shoes."   —Anonymous

    _____

Lesson #18

1 – 3.   Write the six progressive forms of the verb *forget*. Use the subject *I*.

_____
_____
_____
_____
_____
_____

4.   Underline two synonyms in the sentence below.

   If you ask someone to be completely honest, it's a little unfair to be offended by the person's candid remarks.

5.   Add a comma, a semicolon, and an end mark.

   First of all you need to make sure the lettuce is clean you can just rinse it with plenty of cold water

6.   Are any of these plurals misspelled? Use a dictionary to check. Then cross out any misspelled words and write them correctly.

   lillies   mice   fox's

   _____

7. Fill in a pronoun that agrees with the collective noun.

   The company set _____ goals for the next five years.

8. Choose the verb that agrees.

   If anybody (have / has) Lacey's phone number, please call her.

9. Choose the correct form of the adjective.

   From what I've seen, the 2008 model is the (more good / better / best) of the three contenders.

10 – 12. **Identify the Sentence Parts**

The old school house <u>was painted</u> by teen volunteers <u>while</u> the
　　　　　　　　　　　　　A　　　　　　　　　　　　　　B

younger children <u>sold</u> <u>lemonade</u> and <u>worked</u> <u>in</u> the <u>gardens</u>.
　　　　　　　　　C　　　D　　　　　　　E　　F　　　　G

_____ intransitive verb　　　　_____ direct object

_____ passive verb　　　　　　_____ object of a preposition

_____ transitive verb　　　　　_____ preposition

_____ subordinating conjunction

Lesson #19

1. Use context clues to match the meaning of the underlined word.

    The room was filled with cheerful people who were playing games, laughing, and engaging in <u>buoyant</u> conversations.

    strange   repulsive   tranquil   bubbly

2. Underline the transitive verb, circle the indirect object, and put a box around the direct object.

    Aunt Rose gave Kristin an heirloom gold chain.

3. Which spelling is correct?

    _____ probably   _____ probly   _____ neither

4. Correct two capitalization errors with the proper editing marks.

    My Uncle had planned to spend a week on a polynesian island.

5. Underline the correct verb.

    When you (was / were) at Dad's office, did you see his new desk?

6. **A collective noun is singular, and takes a singular verb.**
   Choose the verb that agrees.

    Each class (have / has) its lunch at a different time.

7. Tell whether each clause is subordinate or independent.

    <u>Dad gave me a cell phone</u>; <u>he told me to call</u> <u>whenever I feel lonely</u>.
            A   B   C

    A) _____   B) _____   C) _____

Summer Solutions© Grammar & Writing　　　　　　　　　　　　　　　　　　　　　　　　Level 7

8. Roy is writing a paper about how teenagers choose their friends. He read an article titled "Power Peers" in *New Teen Magazine*. The article was written by Lisa Scott, and it appeared on pages 9 and 10 of the May 2008 edition, Volume 3, Number 5. Show how Roy should cite this reference.

    _____

    _____

9. Write the comparative and superlative form of the adjective.

    few, _____, _____

10. Rewrite the run-on sentence correctly. (Check the *Help Pages* for suggestions.)

    Today's teens choose their friends based on similar interests and values friends may or may not attend the same school.

    _____

    _____

    _____

11 – 12.　**Identify the Sentence Parts**

Older <u>siblings</u> can <u>be</u> positive <u>role models</u>. Many teen-agers <u>who</u>
　　　　　A　　　　　　B　　　　　　C　　　　　　　　　　　　　D

have an older brother or sister say that they have had a <u>better</u> high
　　　　　　　　　　　　　　　　　　　　　　　　　　　　E

school experience <u>because</u> of <u>their</u> sibling relationship.
　　　　　　　　　　F　　　　　　G

_____ subject　　　_____ relative pronoun　　　_____ possessive pronoun

_____ conjunction　_____ linking verb　　　　　_____ predicate nominative

_____ adjective

39

Lesson #20

1. Underline the verb. Then rewrite the sentence using the passive voice of the verb.

   Helen edited my term paper.

   _____

2. Complete this analogy.

   fiction : read : : lemonade : _____

   A) thirst   B) drink   C) beverage   D) sweet

3. The following selection contains a simile or metaphor; which is it? Underline the two things being compared.

   You had better apply early; the application process is as slow as a herd of turtles stampeding through peanut butter.

   simile   metaphor

4. Choose the words that correctly complete the sentence.

   It's a little (to / two / too) early for shorts; (ware /wear) something warmer.

Find an error in each of the following sentences. Cross out the error and write the correction above it. If there is no error, put a star next to the sentence.

Example: The bird has broken ~~it's~~ *its* wing.

5. If we walk quick, we can get to the library before it closes.

6. I reserved a copy of a book called *the Cay* by Theodore Taylor.

7. Also, I want too pick up some DVD's about World War II.

8 – 12. Make a list of your five most indispensable possessions. Then write a sentence about each item, telling why it is so valuable. Write your list and your five sentences below.

Lesson #21

1. Choose the word that has the most appropriate connotation for this sentence.

    Although the small white clusters of flowers are pretty, they have an (unpleasant / abhorrent / obnoxious) smell, so we appreciate them from afar.

2. What type of sentence is used in item 1?

    compound   complex   compound-complex

3. Make the sentence clearer. Cross out the pronoun and replace it with a noun.

    One minute, Bryan was playing with the puppy; then suddenly, he ran away!

4. Make a list of five helping verbs. Check the *Help Pages* if you can't think of five.

    _____

5. Indicate which sentence states a cause and which states an effect.

    A) _____ The August report showed a significant increase in summer merchandise sales.

    B) _____ Consequently, all sales employees will receive gift certificates.

6. Use an editing mark to correct any capitalization errors.

    The circus manager replied, "you'd enjoy a ride on an asian elephant."

Conjugate the irregular verb *cost* in all 14 tenses, using *It* as the subject.

		Past	Present	Future
7.	Basic			
8.	Perfect			
9.	Progressive			
10.	Perfect Progressive			
11.	Emphatic			———

12. Review these word parts by placing them correctly in the chart. Then write an example of a word with each word part.

inter-   *morph*   *-gram*

	Word Part	Meaning	Example
A)		between	
B)		written	
C)		form	

Lesson #22

1. Write the three basic tenses of the verb *apply* with the subject *She*.

    A) _____

    B) _____

    C) _____

2. Choose a synonym for the word *officious*. Use a dictionary if you need help.

    important   hopeful   bossy   attractive

3. Which nouns keep the same form whether singular or plural?

    salmon   child   reindeer   person   scissors

4. Choose the pronoun that makes this meaning clear.

    Actually, Julie likes rocky road ice cream more than (I / me).

5. Which of these is a subordinate clause? _____

    <u>I didn't enjoy the music</u> <u>as much as I enjoyed the story line</u>.
           A   B

6. Underline the adverb; circle the adjective.

    Mrs. Greenway is busy right now, but she will meet with you momentarily.

7. Charlotte has to do a report for Career Day. She interviewed a dental technician named Dave Miller. The interview took place at the office of Dr. Rita Hanson, D.D.S., on May 5, 2011. Show how Charlotte should cite this reference in her bibliography.

    _____

    _____

    _____

8. Choose the correct pronoun (hint: predicate nominative).

   I don't see Lena. Is that (her / she), sitting near the pool?

9. The sentence below has been edited. Rewrite the sentence correctly.

   We're not (aloud) to use roman candles on the Fourth of July.

   _____

   _____

Indicate whether each sentence states a fact or an opinion.

10. _____ According to most insurance companies, a poor driving record increases the price of insurance for the driver with the poor record.

11. _____ Poor drivers should pay higher insurance rates since these drivers typically cost insurance companies more money.

12. _____ Many insurance companies reward accident-free drivers with discounted insurance rates.

Lesson #23

1. Is the underlined word used as a verb or a noun?

    A) The boys won't be working together until their <u>conflict</u> is resolved.

        verb   noun

    B) We painted the walls white, so they won't <u>conflict</u> with the brightly colored fabrics.

        verb   noun

2. Use context clues to match the meaning of the underlined word.

    Since Kevin was such a <u>precocious</u> child, his kindergarten teacher sent him to first grade for reading and math classes.

        bright   annoying   serious   punctual

3. Fill in verbs (was or were) that agree with the subjects of these sentences.

    The community _____ determined to elect a new mayor. Most of the voters _____ extremely dissatisfied with the incumbent.

4. Add the <u>past perfect form</u> of the verb *sing*.

    In previous years, the children's choir _____ _____ holiday carols at a local radio station.

5. Underline the transitive verb, circle the indirect object, and put a box around the direct object.

    I was late, so the teacher gave me a detention.

6. Make the sentence clearer; cross out the pronoun and replace it with a noun. (Hint: What can't be opened — the car, the cooler, or the can of soda?)

    There is a can of soda in the cooler that's in the car, but I can't open it.

7. Choose the words that correctly complete the sentence.

> Kevin's mom wouldn't (accept / except) any money for the baby
>
> (close / clothes) she brought us.

8 – 12. If you could break a world record, which record would you break, and how would you do it? Write a description of at least five sentences.

_____
_____
_____
_____
_____
_____
_____
_____
_____
_____
_____

Lesson #24

1. Complete this analogy. _____ : 212° F :: freezing : boiling

   A) 100° C   B) 98.6° F   C) 32° F   D) temperature

2. Which word has the strongest connotation?

   blunder   faux pas   inaccuracy   mistake

3. Circle the relative pronoun and underline its antecedent.

   Orangutans, monkeys, and gorillas are some of the mammals that live in the rainforests.

4. Match these word parts with their meanings.

   _____ thermo-   _____ omni-   _____ neo-

   A) all   B) heat   C) new

5. Find these words in a thesaurus or dictionary. Choose the word that best completes the sentence.

   curtailed   inconsistent   resolute   parsimonious

   Billie had made up her mind, and she was _____; nothing could stop her from reaching her goal.

6. Choose the correct verb.

   The Temple Mount and The Western Wall (is / are) very sacred places in the Jewish religious tradition.

7. Choose the correct verb for each sentence, and fill it in. (Hint: Use is, are, be, or am.)

   A) Either China or India _____ the most heavily populated country in the world.

   B) Neither Kilimanjaro nor Mount McKinley _____ the world's highest mountain.

8. Underline the compound nouns.

   The candy store sells peanut brittle, sugar canes, and jelly beans.

9 – 12. **Identify the Sentence Parts**

In that small log <u>cabin</u> <u>lived</u> a <u>family</u> called <u>the</u> <u>Murdocks</u>. Each day
                  A   B   C   D   E

Jimmy, <u>the eldest Murdock child</u>, sleepily <u>boarded</u> the <u>school bus</u> at 5 a.m.
               F   G   H

_____ transitive verb   _____ appositive

_____ subject   _____ object of a preposition

_____ direct object   _____ intransitive verb

_____ article   _____ proper noun

Lesson #25

1. Choose the word that correctly completes the sentence.

    A tube passes through the (chute / shoot), and ends up inside the bank at the teller's desk.

2. Write the comparative and superlative form of each adjective.

    high, _____, _____

    sad, _____, _____

3. Use what you know about word parts to match each word with its meaning.

    _____ hydrangea   A) water loving plant

    _____ phobic   B) legal influence

    _____ jurisdiction   C) fearful

4. Underline the demonstrative in this sentence. Is it used as a pronoun or an adjective?

    Yes, I read an article about that in today's newspaper.

    pronoun   adjective

5. Choose the verb that agrees with the indefinite pronoun.

    Think about whether you'd like to see a movie or go to the skating rink; either (are / is) okay with me.

6. Underline the transitive verb, circle the indirect object, and put a box around the direct object.

    At the end of the performance, a jubilant audience gave the cast a standing ovation.

The following selection has some errors. Use it to complete the next two items.

      Setting short-term goals is not very difficult since most people have a pretty good idea of what they want too accomplish. however, reaching a goal is not always that easy. That's why every goal must have a plan to go with it. And a deadline!

7. Cross out a fragment and rewrite it correctly below.

_____

_____

8. Use editing marks to correct two other errors in the selection.

Find an error in each of the following sentences. Cross out the error and write the correction above it. Draw a star next to the sentence if it has no error.

                We've
Example: ~~We~~ been in school together since kindergarten!

9. Tina should of known better than to leave her cell phone on the bus.

10. How was the tigers trained to jump through rings of fire?

11. For who did you arrange a party last week?

12. The kittens got theirselves all tangled up in knitting yarn.

Lesson #26

1. Complete this analogy.   giraffe : spotted :: _____ : wooden

   A) landscape   B) pencil   C) zoo   D) paper

2. Underline the compound nouns; put a double line under the nouns that act as adjectives.

   There are several computer labs in the technology school.

3. Underline the adverb phrase.

   Sean and Tyrell bought chili dogs after the game.

4. In the sentence above, what does the adverb phrase tell?

   how   when   where   why   to what extent

5. Underline the reflexive pronoun; circle its antecedent.

   Theresa and I decided to treat ourselves to lunch at a little Italian pizzeria.

6 – 7.   Match each word with its definition.

   _____ verb   A) action verbs that have a direct object

   _____ transitive   B) action verbs that have no direct object

   _____ intransitive   C) helping

   _____ auxiliary   D) the simple predicate

   _____ forms of *be*   E) the most common linking verbs

8 – 12. Researchers say that about 20% of people living in the United States speak little or no English. What if you wanted to be friends with someone who speaks a different language? What would you do?

_____
_____
_____
_____
_____
_____
_____
_____
_____
_____

Lesson #27

1. Choose an antonym that will change the meaning of the sentence.

    <u>Previously</u>, the documents contained many inconsistencies and errors.

    obviously   undoubtedly   maliciously   subsequently

2. Write the comparative and superlative form of the adjective *attractive*.

    _____, _____

3. Choose the correct pronoun.

    These gloves belong to the person (who / whom) sat next to you at the theater.

4. Underline the transitive verb, circle the indirect object, and put a box around the direct object.

    Jan grilled us a stack of fabulous pancakes.

5. Write the <u>present emphatic form</u> of the verb *play*.

    _____ he _____ jazz?

6. Choose the pronoun and verb that agree with the antecedent.

    Maurice's club is accepting new members. (It is / They are) a rock climbing club.

7. Are any of these plurals misspelled? Use a dictionary to check. Then write any misspelled words correctly.

    snowmen   potatos   shelf's

    _____

8. Choose the words that correctly complete the sentences.

   Many of today's rivers and lakes (is / are) the result of glacial activity. The

   Amazon River (is / are) the largest in terms of the amount of water flow per second.

9. Add the <u>present perfect form</u> of the verb *shine*.

   It's so warm outside; the sun _____ _____

   all day!

10. Underline the linking verb; circle the predicate adjective(s).

    Rachel bought settees for the living room;

    they are really cute and comfortable.

11. Underline the adverb; circle the adjective.

    The beautiful print completed the décor brilliantly.

12. Rewrite the following sentence with the correct capitalization, and insert a colon, quotation marks, and an end mark.

    you have heard this proverb never look a gift horse in the mouth

    _____

    _____

    _____

Lesson #28

1. Complete this analogy.

    letters : words : : notes : _____

    A) speaking   B) English   C) written   D) music

2. What is the denotation of the word *chicken*?

    A) afraid   B) fowl   C) brave   D) cowardly

3. Use what you know about Greek and Latin roots to identify the meaning of *phonology*.

    A) study of sounds   B) single study   C) many sounds   D) fear of sound

4. Which two are synonyms? Use a dictionary to check.

    terrifying   fascinating   convincing   captivating

5. Complete the sentence with a pronoun that agrees with the collective noun.

    The firm moved _____ headquarters to Atlanta, Georgia.

6. Which spelling is correct?

    _____ piece   _____ peice   _____ neither

7. Decide whether the indefinite pronouns are singular or plural. Then choose the verbs that agree.

    During the earthquake, more of the building (was / were) damaged, but most of the windows (is / are) still intact.

Conjugate the irregular verb *feed* in all 14 tenses, using *He* as the subject.

		Past	Present	Future
8.	Basic			
9.	Perfect			
10.	Progressive			
11.	Perfect Progressive			
12.	Emphatic			———

Lesson #29

1. Choose a synonym for the underlined word.

   We need to firm up some details; right now our plan is a little too <u>nebulous</u>.

   lengthy   unclear   exact   risky

2. Use what you know about prefixes and roots to match these words with their meanings.

   _____ polychromatic   A) under ground

   _____ neonate   B) new born

   _____ subterranean   C) many colored

3. How should the underlined part be written? _____

   Let Patricia do the lettering; she engraves more <u>precise than me</u>.

   A) more precise than I.   C) more precisely than I.

   B) preciser than me.   D) correct as is

4. Write an F if the statement is a fact; write O if it is an opinion. Write B if the statement includes both fact and opinion.

   A) _____ Although many school districts are trying to upgrade the nutritional value of school lunches, healthy foods just don't appeal to kids.

   B) _____ A recent survey shows that pizza, hamburgers, and tacos are still the most popular lunch items sold in school cafeterias.

   C) _____ Every kid should have the option of buying a candy bar or some French fries once in a while.

5. Choose the verb that agrees (notice the inverted order).

   Among the many handmade crafts for sale at the fair (was / were) an adorable rag doll.

6. What is the simple subject of the sentence in item 5? _____

7. Underline the transitive verb, circle the indirect object, and put a box around the direct object.

   Mr. Peterson told Dad a joke about the hyenas and elephants.

8. Choose the correct forms.

   If Mark is doing (good / well) in school, why does he feel so (bad / badly)?

9. Does the sentence below contain a simile or a metaphor? Underline the two things that are compared.

   High school is a glorious journey that is much too brief.

   simile   metaphor

10 – 12. Match each word with its definition.

   _____ linking verb   A) has a direct object

   _____ transitive   B) has no direct object

   _____ intransitive   C) can act as auxiliary or linking verbs

   _____ auxiliary   D) helping verb

   _____ forms of *be*   E) connects the subject with a predicate noun or predicate adjective

Lesson #30

1. Complete this analogy.

    script : play : : blueprint : _____

    A) drawing   B) building   C) actors   D) scenery

2. Rewrite the two sentences as a single sentence with an appositive.

    Working at the ice cream stand is my summer job. Working at the ice cream stand is fun and it pays well.

    _____
    _____

3. Insert a comma, quotation marks, and an end mark.

    Maya Angelou said If you find it in your heart to care for somebody else, you will have succeeded

4. Draw a line through two errors in the sentence; then rewrite the sentence correctly.

    Their's an article about the fire in the smorning's newspaper.

    _____
    _____

5. Underline the simple subject; circle the simple predicate.

    Straight-backed penguins, like little cartoons in tuxedos, marched across the tundra with their chicks in tow.

6. Choose the correct verb.

    Do you have any gum? Either spearmint or peppermint (is / are) fine with me.

7. Write the three perfect forms of the verb *wrap* using the subject *She*.

   A) _____

   B) _____

   C) _____

8. Write the comparative and superlative form of the adjective.

   some, _____, _____

9. Sort the nouns into two categories: collective and compound.

   Mount Everest   team   side street   flock   crowd   guest house

   collective - _____

   compound - _____

10 – 12. **Identify the Sentence Parts**

Lila, Rebecca's little sister, will perform at the piano recital
          A   B   C

on Labor Day. Please give her as much support as you can.
    D   E   F

_____ prepositional phrase   _____ direct object

_____ verb phrase   _____ compound noun

_____ appositive   _____ indirect object

Level 7

English Grammar & Writing Mechanics

Help Pages

Help Pages

The Eight Parts of Speech
Adjectives modify nouns or pronouns. A proper adjective begins with a capital letter.
Adverbs modify verbs, adjectives, or other adverbs. Adverbs tell *how*, *when*, *where*, and *to what extent*.
Conjunctions connect similar words, clauses, or phrases within a sentence.
Coordinate Conjunctions: and, or, nor, but, yet, for, so
Subordinating Conjunctions join a subordinate clause with a main clause. (See the chart below.)
Correlative Conjunctions act in pairs.   either/or, neither/nor, both/and, whether/or, not/but, not only/but also
Interjections are words or phrases that express strong feeling. **Examples:** Ouch! Gosh! Oh no!
Nouns name a person, place, thing, or idea. Nouns may be common or proper, singular or plural, abstract or concrete. A proper noun begins with a capital letter.
Collective Nouns are words that name a "collection." A collective noun is singular and is treated as a single unit. <u>Collective nouns</u> used as subjects take <u>singular verbs</u>.   **Examples:** the <u>family</u> *is*, the <u>orchestra</u> *plays*, a <u>committee</u> *studies*
Prepositions relate nouns or pronouns to other words in the sentence. For a list of common prepositions, see the chart below.
Prepositional Phrases begin with a preposition and end with a <u>noun</u> or a <u>pronoun</u>.   **Examples:** *against* the <u>fence</u>, *beside* <u>me</u>
Pronouns replace nouns. The pronoun *I* is always capitalized.   Common pronoun types are described on p. 67.
Verbs convey action or a state of being. A verb is the main word in the predicate of a sentence. For an explanation of verb types, see p. 67.

Subordinating Conjunctions

after	as much as	even if	in order that	than, that	when
although	as soon as	even though	now that	though	whenever
as	as though	how	provided	till	where
as if	because	if	since	unless	wherever
as long as	before	inasmuch as	so that	until	while

Common Prepositions

about	around	down	instead of	out	toward
above	before	during	into	outside	under
across	behind	except	near	over	underneath
across from	below	for	nearby	past	until
after	beneath	from	next to	since	up
against	beside	in	of	through	upon
along	between	in back of	off	throughout	with
alongside	beyond	in front of	on	to	within
among	by	inside	onto	together with	without

Help Pages

Editing Marks

Capitalize	≡	Take something out	⌐
Add end punctuation	⊙ ❓ ❗	Check spelling	sp
Add something	∧	Indent	¶
Make lower case	/		

Abbreviations

There are four types of abbreviations (see below). Notice that some abbreviations are capitalized and some are not. Some abbreviations require a period; some do not. Consult a dictionary for the correct way to write an abbreviation.

Avoid using abbreviations in formal writing.

1. Shortened words: in. (inch)   Corp. (Corporation)   limo (limousine)
2. Contractions: Dr. (Doctor)   didn't (did not)   tsp. (teaspoon)
3. Initials: LTD   U.S.A.   R & R
4. Acronyms: LASER   PETA   MADD

Rules for Using Brackets, Colons, Semicolons, Dashes, and Hyphens

Brackets [ ] are used in dictionary definitions or to insert words into writing that is already within parentheses. Brackets are always used in pairs.

Colons: 1. A colon (:) is used between the hour and minutes, or between minutes and seconds when writing the time.
   Examples: At around 12:30, we eat lunch.
        My running time was 13:35 (13 minutes and 35 seconds).
  2. A colon may be used after the greeting in a formal or business letter.
  3. A colon may be used before a list of items, but never after a preposition or a verb.
   Incorrect ➔ I have traveled to: Russia, Italy, Iran, and Cuba.
   Correct ➔ I have visited many countries: Russia, Italy, Iran, and Cuba.
  4. A colon may be used before a long quote or if there is no other introduction, such "he said" or "she replied."
   Example: Martha looked up at George: "Where have you been all day?"

Semicolons: 1. A semicolon (;) may be used to separate two independent clauses with no conjunction. The semicolon takes the place of a comma or conjunction.
   Incorrect ➔ You can come in now; but please sit quietly.
   Correct ➔ You can come in now; please sit quietly.
  2. Use a semicolon to separate items in a series if there are already commas in the items.
   Example: Lorain, Ohio; New Castle, Pennsylvania; and Chicago, Illinois

Dashes (—) are used between words within sentences. A dash is longer than a hyphen and is used to show emphasis. A dash should be used for a special effect — do not overuse it.

Help Pages

Rules for using Hyphens
1. Use a hyphen between the tens and the ones place, when writing out the numbers twenty-one through ninety-nine. **Examples:** forty-two   seventy-six
2. Use a hyphen when writing fractions. **Example:** three-fifths   two-thirds
3. Use a hyphen to separate words on two lines. The word must be separated by syllables, and each syllable should have at least two letters. (Whenever possible, avoid separation of words in this way.)
4. Use a hyphen to join a prefix with a base word. The hyphen helps make the word more clear. **Examples:** co-captains   ex-mayor   non-taxable
5. Use a hyphen in some compound words. **Examples:** well-rounded   president-elect
6. Words are changing and are being added to the English language constantly. Therefore, always use an up-to-date dictionary to verify whether or not a word can should be hyphenated.

Rules for using Commas
1. Use commas to separate words or phrases in a series. **Example**: Sun brought a coloring book, some crayons, a pair of scissors, and a ruler.
2. Use a comma to separate two independent clauses joined by a conjunction. **Example**: Dad works in the city, and he is a commuter.
3. Use a comma after an introductory word, such as an interjection. **Example**: Hey, who wants to play tennis? Do not use a comma if there is an end mark after the interjection. **Example**: Oh no! It's starting to rain.
4. Use a comma to separate consecutive words or numbers when writing a date. **Example**: Friday, April 7, 2006
5. Use commas between adjectives if the order doesn't matter. **Example**: the exciting, fresh dance moves (This could also written "fresh, exciting dance moves" or "exciting and fresh dance moves.")
6. Do not use commas between adjectives that describe in different ways. **Example**: three green tomatoes   (Three tells how many, and green describes the color.)
7. Insert a comma after introductory words or phrases in a sentence. **Example**: On the other hand, you may not need any help.
8. Use commas before and after interrupting phrases within a sentence. **Example**: Ms. Cole, the bank teller, was very helpful.
9. Use commas before and/or after contrasting phrases that use *not*. **Example**: I worked on my science project, not my essay, all evening.

Help Pages

Sentences			
Sentence Types: Declarative, Exclamatory, Interrogative, and Imperative			
Structure	**Parts**	**Joined by**	**Example**
Simple	subject and predicate	————	Winter is a great time to try downhill skiing.
Compound	two or more independent clauses	coordinate conjunction (and, but, or)	You can use your own skis, *or* you can rent all your gear at a ski resort.
Complex	subordinate and main clause	subordinating conjunction	You may want to do some sledding *if* downhill skiing is too scary.
Compound-Complex	two or more main clauses and one or more subordinate clauses	conjunctions (both coordinate and subordinating)	Snowboarding is also lots of fun, *and* it's pretty easy *as long as* you have good balance.

Verbs
Action Verbs show action or possession.

Transitive Verbs are action verbs that send action to a direct object.
         Example: Pat *reads* the newspaper every morning.
         (verb - reads; direct object - newspaper)

Intransitive Verbs are action verbs that have no direct object.   **Example:** Pat *reads* all the time. (verb - reads; no direct object)
Verbs of Being (forms of *be*) do not show action; they can act as linking or helping verbs.   is, are, was, were, be, am, being, been
Linking Verbs do not show action; they show a condition.   appear, become, feel, seem, smell, taste, sound, and all forms of *be*.

Auxiliary (Helping) Verbs are used with other verbs to form a verb phrase.
     is, are, was, were, be, am, being, been, might, could, should, would,
     can, do, does, did, may, must, will, shall, have, has, had

Verb Tense tells the time when the action or condition of the verb occurs. There are fourteen tenses (see the verb conjugation chart on page 71). The <u>basic</u> verb tenses are past, present, and future.

Pronouns
Demonstrative Pronouns are used to point out something.   this, that, these, those   Demonstratives can also be adjectives.   **Examples:** *this* dog, *these* people
Interrogative Pronouns are used to ask a question   what, which, who, whom, whose
Nominative Pronouns are used as the subject or as a predicate nominative.   I, you, he, she, it, we, you, they
Object Pronouns are used in the predicate as a direct object or an object of a preposition.   me, you, him, her, it, us, them, whom

Possessive Pronouns show ownership. Some possessive pronouns are used with nouns.
     my, your, his, her, its, our, your, their, whose
     Other possessive pronouns can stand alone: hers, his, mine, ours, theirs, yours, and whose.

Relative Pronouns are used to relate a clause to an antecedent.   that, which, who, whom, whose

Help Pages

Pronouns (Cont'd)
Indefinite Pronouns replace nouns that are not specific.
Singular: another, each, everything, nobody, other, anybody, either, little, no one, somebody, anyone, everybody, much, nothing, someone, anything, everyone, neither, one, something
Plural: both, few, many, others, several
Singular and Plural: all, any, more, most, none, some
Spelling Rules
Rules for Forming Plurals
1. Words ending in *s*, *x*, *z*, *ch*, or *sh*, add *-es* to make the plural.
2. Many words that end in *-f* or *-fe* form the plural by changing the *-f* or *-fe* to *-ves* (thief - thieves). Some nouns that end in *-f* or *-ff* do not follow the rule for making plurals. (cliff - cliffs, belief - beliefs).
3. Some nouns that end in a consonant + *-o* form the plural by adding *-s* (tattoo - tattoos); others add *-es* (veto - vetoes).
4. Some nouns do not add *-s* or *-es* to form the plural; these irregular plurals must be memorized (phenomenon - phenomena).
5. Some nouns have the same form whether they are singular or plural (deer, grapefruit, salmon).
6. Some nouns have only a plural form, and they always take a plural verb (scissors, pants, dues).
7. Some nouns are singular even though they end in *-s*; they take singular verbs (mumps, economics, atlas).
Other Spelling Rules
8. Place *i* before *e*, except after *c*, or when sounded like *ā* as in *neighbor* and *weigh* (mischief, eight).
9. Regular verbs show past tense by adding *-ed* (stop - stopped). Irregular verbs change their spelling in the past tense. See the Irregular Verbs chart on p. 69.
10. When adding a prefix to a word, do not change the spelling of the prefix or the root (*mis-* + step → misstep).
11. If a word ends in a vowel + *-y*, add a suffix without changing the spelling of the word (employ + *-er* → employer).
12. If a word ends in a consonant + *-y*, change the *y* to *i* before adding suffixes such as *-es*, *-er*, *-ed*, or *-est* (try - tried). If the suffix begins with an *-i*, do not change the *-y* to *-i* (hurry - hurrying).

Help Pages

Irregular Verbs			
Present	**Present Participle**	**Past**	**Past Participle**
bet	betting	bet	*has*, *have*, or *had* bet
burn	burning	burned/burnt	*has*, *have*, or *had* burned/burnt
cost	costing	cost	*has*, *have*, or *had* cost
dig	digging	dug	*has*, *have*, or *had* dug
dive	diving	dived/dove	*has*, *have*, or *had* dived
feed	feeding	fed	*has*, *have*, or *had* fed
find	finding	found	*has*, *have*, or *had* found
forget	forgetting	forgot	*has*, *have*, or *had* forgotten
hang	hang	hung	*has*, *have*, or *had* hung
kneel	kneeling	knelt	*has*, *have*, or *had* knelt
lay	laying	laid	*has*, *have*, or *had* laid
let	letting	let	*has*, *have*, or *had* let
meet	meeting	met	*has*, *have*, or *had* met
pay	paying	paid	*has*, *have*, or *had* paid
rise	rising	rose	*has*, *have*, or *had* risen
seek	seeking	sought	*has*, *have*, or *had* sought
send	sending	sent	*has*, *have*, or *had* sent
shed	shedding	shed	*has*, *have*, or *had* shed
spend	spending	spent	*has*, *have*, or *had* spent
strike	striking	struck	*has*, *have*, or *had* struck
swell	swelling	swelled	*has*, *have*, or *had* swelled / swollen
upset	upsetting	upset	*has*, *have*, or *had* upset
win	winning	won	*has*, *have*, or *had* won
withstand	withstanding	withstood	*has*, *have*, or *had* withstood

Prefixes, Suffixes, and Roots (Oh my!)							
	Meaning		**Meaning**		**Meaning**		**Meaning**
able	able to	*de*	take away	*mal*	evil	*port*	carry
amphi	both	*di*	two	*micro*	tiny	*post*	after
ante	before	*dia*	across	*mis*	badly	*pre*	before
anthropo	human	*dict*	speak	*mono*	one	*re*	again
anti	against	*dis*	not	*morph*	form	*scrib*	write
auto	self	*ful*	full of	*neo*	new	*script*	write
biblio	book	*geo*	earth	*non*	not	*sub*	under
bi	two	*graph, gram*	written	*ology*	study of	*super*	above
bio	life	*hemi*	half	*omni*	all	*thermo*	heat
bronte	thunder	*hydro*	water	*ped*	foot	*trans*	across
centri	center	*ible*	able	*phobe*	fear	*tri*	three
circum	around	*im, in*	not	*phobia*	fear	*un*	not
co, com	with	*inter*	between	*phone*	sound		
con	with	*jur, jus, jud*	law	*photo*	light		
chrono	time	*less*	without	*poly*	many		

Help Pages

Bibliography
A bibliography is a list of sources that were used in the preparation of a research document. The bibliography is arranged in alphabetical order by author's name. The title of the book, magazine, or Internet article is included, as well as the publisher, date of publication, and sometimes page numbers. Bibliography styles may differ slightly, and you should follow your teacher's specific directions for setting up your bibliography. Here are some guidelines and examples of how to list various sources. The following use MLA format. **Some of the information listed here may not be available. If the information is not available, just include as much as you can in the citation.**

Book with One Author:
    Author's Last name, First name. Title of Book. City: Publisher, Date.
Example:
    Lawry, Matthew. Fascinating Desert Life Forms. Dayton: Traders Press, 2004.

Book with Two or Three Authors:
    Author's Last name, First name and additional author's First and Last name(s). Title of Book.
        City: Publisher, Date.
Example:
    Morris, Paul, Trudy Willis, and Marie Jenson. Hiker Meets Cactus. Chicago: Toads Press, 2008.

Encyclopedia:
    Author's Last name, First name. "Title of Article." Title of Encyclopedia.
        City: Publisher, year ed.
Example:
    Hernandez, Noreen. "Arid Biomes." Universe Encyclopedia. New York: Green, Inc., 2006 ed.

Magazine Article:
    Author's Last name, First name. "Article Title." Title of Magazine Month year: page numbers.
Example:
    Parched, Sandy. "My Days in the Sahara." Geography and More March 2000: 23-29.

Internet Article:
    Author's Last name, First name. "Article Title." Website Title. Date of posting or date of last
        update. Site sponsor. Date you visited the website. <web address>.
Example:
    Greenberg, Tasha. "Desert Life." Topics to Research. March 2006. International
        Geographics. Sept. 16, 2010. <http://topicstoresearch.com/biomes/desert.html>.

Website with No Author:
    "Site Title." Sponsor. Copyright date or latest update. Date you visited the website.
        <web address>.
Example:
    "Desert Days." Environments Global. 2009. Aug. 23, 2010.
        <http://environsglobal.net/days/desert.html>.

Personal Interview:
    Person's Last name, First name. Kind of interview (personal interview or phone call). Date of
        interview.
Example:
    Jogan, James. Personal interview. February 20, 2007.

Help Pages

Complete Verb Conjugation		
A complete verb conjugation shows all 14 tenses with the singular and plural nominative pronouns. Below is the complete conjugation chart for the <u>irregular</u> verb *forget*.		
Verb Form	**Singular**	**Plural**
Past	I forgot. You forgot. He / She / It forgot.	We forgot. You forgot. They forgot.
Present	I forget. You forget. He / She / It forgets.	We forget. You forget. They forget.
Future	I will forget. You will forget. He / She / It will forget.	We will forget. You will forget. They will forget.
Past Perfect	I had forgotten. You had forgotten. He / She / It had forgotten.	We had forgotten. You had forgotten. They had forgotten.
Present Perfect	I have forgotten. You have forgotten. He / She / It has forgotten.	We have forgotten. You have forgotten. They have forgotten.
Future Perfect	I will have forgotten. You will have forgotten. He / She / It will have forgotten.	We will have forgotten. You will have forgotten. They will have forgotten.
Past Progressive	I was forgetting. You were forgetting. He / She / It was forgetting.	We were forgetting. You were forgetting. They were forgetting.
Present Progressive	I am forgetting. You are forgetting. He / She / It is forgetting.	We are forgetting. You are forgetting. They are forgetting.
Future Progressive	I will be forgetting. You will be forgetting. He / She / It will be forgetting.	We will be forgetting. You will be forgetting. They will be forgetting.
Past Perfect Progressive	I had been forgetting. You had been forgetting. He / She / It had been forgetting.	We had been forgetting. You had been forgetting. They had been forgetting.
Present Perfect Progressive	I have been forgetting. You have been forgetting. He / She / It has been forgetting.	We have been forgetting. You have been forgetting. They have been forgetting.
Future Perfect Progressive	I will have been forgetting. You will have been forgetting. He / She / It will have been forgetting.	We will have been forgetting. You will have been forgetting. They will have been forgetting.
Emphatic Past	I did forget. You did forget. He / She / It did forget.	We did forget. You did forget. They did forget.
Emphatic Present	I do forget. You do forget. He / She / It does forget.	We do forget. You do forget. They do forget.

Help Pages

How to Fix a Run-on Sentence
A **run-on sentence** has two or more independent clauses which are not properly joined. **Example:** Today we had planned to go on a picnic it rained all afternoon!

- **Separate two independent clauses into two sentences.**   Today we had planned to go on a picnic. It rained all afternoon!

- **Insert a semicolon between the two independent clauses.**   Today we had planned to go on a picnic; it rained all afternoon!

- **Insert a semicolon between the two independent clauses and add a transitional word (*therefore, moreover, for example*, etc.) and a comma.**   Today we had planned to go on a picnic; however, it rained all afternoon!

- **Insert a comma and a coordinating conjunction between the two independent clauses.**   Today we had planned to go on a picnic, but it rained all afternoon!

- **Rewrite the sentence using a subordinating conjunction to separate the two independent clauses.**   Although we had planned to go on a picnic today, it rained all afternoon!

Level 7

English Grammar
& Writing Mechanics

Answers to Lessons

Lesson #1		Lesson #2		Lesson #3	
1	damp	1	<u>you</u> are traveling	1	✓ one, or single
2	(lay) the most unique train set Brian had ever seen.	2	<u>weather update</u> <u>Death Valley</u> <u>Morning Report</u>	2	~~S~~pring ~~M~~om grandpa alaskan
3	(lived) a lonely little troll	3	<u>as long as there are no customers</u>	3	poorly challenging
4	difference	4	verb, adjective, or adverb	4	lit The candles were lit by Ken.
5	<u>tour guide</u> <u>Zany World</u>	5	B	5	As long as there is no lightning,…
6	completely gradually chiefly	6	The marathon, an annual event, is…	6	~~memo's~~ memos
7	swell swelled swelling swelled	7	Answers will vary.	7	(lady) <u>whom</u>
8	…intelligent, honest, friendly, and…	8	Seals dive. Seals will dive.	8	subordinate
9	cautious	9	Seals had dived. Seals have dived.	9	clear
10	~~they do not require~~ it does not require	10	Seals are diving. Seals will be diving.	10-12	Answers will vary.
11-12	E F C D A B	11	Seals had been diving. Seals will have been diving.		
		12	Seals did dive. Seals do dive.		

Summer Solutions© Grammar & Writing — Level 7

	Lesson #4		Lesson #5		Lesson #6
1	…the team; as soon as…	1	Answers will vary.	1	…bananas. her…
2	ballet teacher / carrot cake / dance recital	2	café owner apple pie	2	copy machine / technology specialist
3	gave (drummers) [ovation]	3	after a storm look	3	while she stirred told the pudding
4	Until I graduated from high school,	4	had raked	4	A) ✓ both B) ✓ transitive
5	prosperous / affluent	5	…snack, not a meal,…	5	The Wilsons' house, a two-story colonial, has a full basement.
6	It's too wear	6	whose	6	dad jefferson lake
7	Everyone her	7	easter grandma cornish	7	A
8	impolite	8–11	Colleges offer summer programs to seventh and eighth graders for a variety of reasons. ~~Like robotics or debate.~~ ~~And a chance to meet other kids like themselves.~~ ~~are~~ is ~~prefers~~ prefer ~~allow~~ allows (coarses)sp (envirament)sp	8	C A B
9	a fire			9	were
10	Answers will vary.			10	All of the baby zoo animals
11–12	C / B / A / D			11	(incase) (yous) Take your cell phone in case any of you need to call home.
		12	A	12	Doing odd jobs, mowing lawns, and babysitting are just a few of the ways to earn extra cash this summer.

	Lesson #7		Lesson #8		Lesson #9
1	✓ includes all forms of *be* ✓ does not show action	1	(1 – 3, examples will vary.) *trans*- transfer transport	1	A) when B) where C) how D) to what extent
2	Answers may vary. See Help Pages for a complete list.	2	*anti*- anticeptic anticlimatic	2	power, raisins, tricycle
3	(is) home	3	*ante*- antecedent antebellum	3	Louise, Mr. Norris, Virginia
4	lightly	4	during our rehearsal	4	has shed
5	room oven simile	5	so that the room adjust is shaded	5	complex
6	Did (you) send	6	P A	6	hangs (painting)
7	you ~~yourself~~	7	Okay,...submitted, but it's...Wednesday, April 10.	7	A P
8	has won	8	abundant scarce	8 - 12	(Wording may vary.) cat climbed up Christmas tree; tree started to fall I caught the tree; bent the tree stand pushed on stand to straighten tree; I shook tree; spooked the cat cat jumped off tree; spilled lemonade
9	A C B	9	gave (Glenda) [photos]		
10	A) O B) F	10	is		
11 - 12	B C D G F A E	11	S: license, forest, weather P: donuts, clouds, people		
		12	Shock, Walter. <u>Careers in Gaming</u>. Toronto: Roulette Press, 2006.		

Summer Solutions© Grammar & Writing — Level 7

	Lesson #10		Lesson #11		Lesson #12
1	Flip-flops are comfortable, but it isn't sensible to wear them in the winter.	1	D	1	We had sought. We have sought. We will have sought.
2	A - devotion, confidence, safety C - hot dogs, magazine, camel	2	<u>hoover</u> <u>dam</u> <u>lake</u> <u>mead</u> <u>nevada</u>	2	A
3	B	3	unusual	3	adjective
4	…everything: canoeing, skiing, biking, and…	4	<u>storage room</u> <u>museum</u> metaphor	4	B C A
5	<u>hope</u> <u>air</u> metaphor	5	had forgotten	5	My favorite breakfast, French toast, is on the menu.
6	C	6	(is) locked	6	~~him~~ Don
7	all	7	transitive	7	A
8	✓ locally	8	A) fact B) opinion	8	your
9	its	9-12	Answers will vary.	9	that were not even functional
10-12	will: Helping Future go: Action Present are: Linking Present give: Action Present look: Linking Present			10	~~G~~randmother <u>german</u>
				11-12	C E B D A F

Lesson #13	Lesson #14	Lesson #15
1. P A	1. pay paid paying has/have/had paid	1. bitter
2. D	2. <u>colossal</u> <u>petite</u>	2. will have hung
3. C A B	3. phenomenon	3. a lot drowned probably
4. ✓ February	4. C	4. burns promotes
5. is	5. <u>the golden compass</u>	5. this pronoun
6. <u>Olympic medal</u> <u>day camp</u> <u>Mr. Holmes</u>	6. whom	6. has
7. B	7. was were	7. phrase
8. The batter struck. The batter strikes. The batter will strike.	8. Gardens, Daisy. <u>Landscaping Careers</u>. Chicago: Greens Press, 2006.	8. over any large (stones) or with the (lawn mower)
9. The batter had struck. The batter has struck. The batter will have struck.	9. quickly	9. you ~~yourself~~
10. The batter was striking. The batter is striking. The batter will be striking.	10. Mason is on the student council and wants to be class president.	10. were ~~was~~
11. The batter had been striking. The batter has been striking. The batter will have been striking.	11. compound-complex	11. its ~~it's~~
12. The batter did strike. The batter does strike	12. compound	12. smallest ~~smaller~~

Lesson #16		Lesson #17		Lesson #18	
1	A) He had been mopping. B) He has been mopping. C) He will have been mopping.	1	upset upset upsetting 　　　　　　has/had/ have upset	1 - 3	I was forgetting. I am forgetting. I will be forgetting. I had been forgetting. I have been forgetting. I will have been forgetting.
2	D	2	impolite		
3	B C A	3	lilies, carnations, roses,		
4	<u>wall</u> <u>blank canvas</u> metaphor	4	C A B	4	<u>honest</u> <u>candid</u>
5	tastes supplies	5	are	5	First of all, you need to make sure the lettuce is clean; you…water.
6	astutely logically luckily	6	passive	6	~~lillies~~ ~~fox's~~ lilies foxes
7	"let's… italian… 　≡　　　≡	7	B　　　C A	7	its
8	~~hisself~~ himself	8	~~they serve~~ it serves	8	has
9	adjourns	9	P C	9	best
10	winds	10	<u>that we heard</u> music	10 - 12	E　　　D A　　　G C　　　F B
11	"Claustrophobia." <u>Minds Encyclopedia</u>. 2001: 33.	11	complex		
12	(their)^sp ~~S~~ummer	12	compound-complex		

	Lesson #19		Lesson #20		Lesson #21
1	bubbly	1	<u>edited</u> My term paper was edited by Helen.	1	unpleasant
2	gave (Kristin) [chain]	2	B	2	compound-complex
3	✓ probably	3	<u>application process</u> <u>herd of turtles</u> simile	3	~~he~~ the puppy (or Bryan)
4	U̶ncle <u>polynesian</u>	4	too wear	4	Answers may vary. See Help Pages for a complete list.
5	were	5	quickly ~~quick~~	5	A) cause B) effect
6	has	6	The ~~the~~	6	you'd <u>asian</u>
7	A) independent B) independent C) subordinate	7	to ~~too~~	7	It cost. It costs. It will cost.
8	Scott, Lisa, "Power Peers." <u>New Teen Magazine</u> May 2008: 9 – 10.			8	It had cost. It has cost. It will have cost.
9	fewer, fewest			9	It was costing. It is costing. It will be costing
10	Answers will vary.	8 - 12	Answers will vary.	10	It had been costing. It has been costing. It will have been costing.
11 - 12	A D G F B C E			11	It did cost. It does cost.
				12	A) *inter-* B) *-gram* C) *morph* (Examples will vary.)

	Lesson #22		Lesson #23		Lesson #24
1	A) She applied. B) She applies. C) She will apply.	1	A) noun B) verb	1	C
2	bossy	2	bright	2	blunder
3	salmon reindeer scissors	3	was were	3	mammals (that)
4	I	4	had sung	4	B A C
5	B	5	gave (me) detention	5	resolute
6	(busy) right now momentarily	6	it̶ the car *or* the cooler *or* the can	6	are
7	Miller, David. Personal interview. May 5, 2008.	7	accept clothes	7	A) is B) is
8	she	8 - 12	Answers will vary.	8	candy store peanut brittle sugar canes jelly beans
9	We're not allowed to use Roman candles on the Fourth of July.			9 - 12	G F C A H B D E
10	fact				
11	opinion				
12	fact				

Lesson #25		Lesson #26		Lesson #27	
1	chute	1	B	1	subsequently
2	higher, highest sadder, saddest	2	<u>computer</u> labs <u>technology</u> school	2	more attractive most attractive
3	A C B	3	after the game.	3	who
4	<u>that</u> pronoun	4	when	4	<u>grilled</u> (us) stack
5	is	5	(Theresa and I) ourselves	5	Does play
6	<u>gave</u> (cast) ovation	6-7	D A B C E	6	It is
7	~~And a deadline!~~ Answers will vary.			7	potatoes shelves
8	(too)^sp <u>however</u>	8-12	Answers will vary.	8	are is
9	should've (should have) ~~should of~~			9	has shone
10	were ~~was~~			10	<u>are</u> (cute) (comfortable)
11	whom ~~who~~			11	(beautiful) <u>brilliantly</u>
12	themselves ~~theirselves~~			12	You have heard this proverb: "Never look a gift horse in the mouth."

Lesson #28		Lesson #29		Lesson #30	
1	D	1	unclear	1	B
2	B	2	C B A	2	Working at the ice cream stand, my summer job, is fun and pays well. (Answers may vary.)
3	A	3	C	3	Maya Angelou said, "If you find…succeeded."
4	fascinating captivating	4	A) B B) F C) O	4	~~Their's the smorning's~~ There's this morning's
5	its	5	was	5	penguins (marched)
6	✓ piece	6	ragdoll	6	is
7	was are	7	told (Dad) [joke]	7	She had wrapped. She has wrapped. She will have wrapped.
8	He fed. He feeds. He will feed.	8	well bad	8	more, most
9	He had fed. He has fed. He will have fed.	9	High school journey metaphor	9	col – team, flock, crowd com – Mount Everest, side street, guest house
10	He was feeding. He is feeding. He will be feeding.	10-12	E A B D C	10-12	D F B C A E
11	He had been feeding. He has been feeding. He will have been feeding.				
12	He did feed. He does feed.				